Loving Autumn

Emily Winter

ISBN 9798457570733

Cover art by Megan Lindsey

Photos by Casey Olsen, Jonnelle Yankovich (p. 6), Aditya Joshi (p. 10), Annie Spratt (p.12), Hanna Balan (p.14), Max Chan (p.21), Kira Auf Der Heide (p.22), Erica Marsland (p.28), Quentin Zwzeor (p.30, 35), Sonny Mauricio (p.38), Daniel J Schwarz (p.46), Olivia Hutcherson (p.49), Xiaolong Wong (p.50), Branden Skeli (p.53), Alexander Sinn (p.57), Luke Porter (p.62), Daniel J Schwarz (p. 68), Gokhan Ayar (p.80), Mohammed Ajwad (p.88).

Printed in the United States of America

CONTENTS

Autumn Winds

Autumn winds fill my senses,
bringing childhood memories with it,
ones I wish I could reach out and take
to relive them once again.

Back to times of euphoria, invincibility,
days with no end,
just a beating, playful heart
welcoming adventure,
a love that hangs on eternity.

I only stop for a moment,
as I hear a voice through the aged,
screen door, calling me into
a warm home with aromas of
nutmeg and cinnamon.

Those times are only a whisper now,
somewhere deep, far, and locked away,
only to flicker in the dark,
whenever I look at falling leaves,
at autumn winds.

Blue Jay

Your call awakens times as a child,
when I walked down a road
of cracks and crumbles,
my gaze on a lonely park,
its swings paint-chipped and weathered.

I had just emerged from the forest,
heart wild from imagination,
like I had just returned from
some far off place,
searching for a friend I could not see,
but knew was there listening.

You're the sound of fall, warning me the season's changing, sending euphoria throughout my being, igniting a heart to treasure the moment, to tune into whispers of nature.

Cinnamon

Many hands have held you
to season their lives,
but little did they know
they inspired their children
to always remember them by.

Under the Apple Tree

Playful, laughing,
gathering a harvest so plentiful
into a woven basket,
I hold an apple in my hand.
Its hue is so rich and taste so sweet,
a look into the heavenly scene
my dear sweet autumn brings.

I'm so glad you're here with me to
enjoy these little things.

Pumpkins

Here you are again,
welcoming me to a season
of gray, fogged mornings and
warm fires inside from
the pouring rain.

Whether on the mantle,
or amidst the amber leaves,
or paired with plum shaded mums
atop the aged porch steps,
you fit in just fine here,
a small but special part of
this autumn scene,
where I'll spend such precious times
that will live on in my memory.

You're a touch of hope after
the hardships of this year,
a simple, raw gift,
a harvest from hard work,
a reminder of the joy in simple things.

With the Morning

On a cold, October morning,
when it's still dark and blue,
I let the air consume me
with tranquility, with love,
and assurance i'll pull through.

I feel special in this moment,
just before the world wakes,
like nature's focus is on me,
eager to converse and
help me feel new.

...nmchen *Pholiota mutabilis* (Schff. ex Fr.) Quél.

Familie: Düanblättler

Tribu: Schüpplingartige (*Pholiotae*)

...unter. Der Hut dieses Laubholzbewohners hat im frischen Zustand eine ...wäßrte und dadurch dunklere Randzone. Beim Austrocknen nimmt er von ...hen nach außen fortschreitend eine viel hellere Ockerfarbe an. Die gebuckelte ...lich ist feuchtigkeit schmierig an. Die Oberhaut ist glatt und fühlt sich etwas fettig, bei ...ren (vergl. auch Nr. 21) kakaobraunen. Die blaßbraunen Lamellen werden durch die reifenden ...llen braunkraube. Der Stiel ist mit abstehenden Schüppchen besetzt, die bis ...au der Haut herauftreichen, welche den Stiel mit dem Hutrand verbindet und an ...erwachsene Pilz als Stielring erhalten bleibt. Im Stiel ist es dunkler und faserigzäh ...bräunliche Farbe und warzigen Geruch. Vom Mai als Vorliebe für die ...vorkommen. Das Stockschwämmchen hat eine ausgeprägte Vorliebe für die ...Stümpfe der Buchen und anderer Laubbäume, über die mit den Pilzen besetzt sind der ...fetten Holzbewohnern. Auch an Laubbäumen, die über und über mit den Pilzen besetzt sind ...au Pappel- und Erlenstümpfen, die über und über mit den Pilzen bestellt sind Ernten ...einen hübschen Anblick bieten. Eine reizende Ausnahme bilden die Vorkommen dieser ...Art auf Nadelholz. Aber die Büschel erreichen hier nicht zu großen Umfang ...Wert. Das Stockschwämmchen wird auf lockenden Böden so gehäuft ...schützt. Auch gebraten entwickelt es ein kräftiges, angenehmes Aroma. Wenn auch ...an einzelnen dünnen Hütchen nicht viel dran ist, so tritt der Pilz doch so gehäuft ...auf, daß ein einziger Baumstumpf eine reichliche Mahlzeit liefern kann. Bein Ein- ...sammeln lade man die zähen Stiele gleich draußen. Lamellen und Hutkaut werden ...mitverwendet. Das verlangt aber, daß alle Verunreinigungen durch Humus, Holz- ...teilchen usw., sorgfältig beseitigt werden müssen.

Verwandte: Die zahlreichen noch zierlicheren Vertreter der Gattung Schüppling

• *(Pholiota)* an Holz und auf dem Erdboden kümmer für den Praktiker schon ...gar nicht in Betracht. Unter den größeren, meist ebenfalls büschelig wachsenden ...Arten gibt es auffallend freudig gefärbte, stark schnippschützige. Hier sei nur zur ...Sparrige Schüppling *Pholiota squarrosa* (Müll.) Quél. erwähnt, der zur ...Herbstzeit in dicken Büscheln mit Vorliebe am Grunde lebender Obstbäume hervor- ...bricht. Als Spezepilz ist er minderwertig. Andere Arten besiedeln sogar in mehreren ...Metern Höhe die absterbenden Äste und Stämme. Man verwechsle das Stockschwäm- ...chen nicht mit ähnlich wachsenden Schwefelköpfen, von denen die bitter schmecken- ...den ungenießbar sind. (Vgl. Bd. II, Tf. 17).

30

The Plaid Blanket

The wooden chest creaks as
I'm on my knees, lifting it's lid,
welcoming my senses once again
to the savory aromas of years before
of faint apple spice and aged cinnamon.

Inside is my plaid blanket, perfectly folded.
It's crimson and navy stripes
whisper to me the fall season is in motion,
ready to accompany me in the chilling wind,
the land stained with rain.

I hold it in front of me. It breathes.
Over my shoulders it goes, covering
all but my leather boots below, which
tread along the pine floors
and outside the front door.

A sea of faded rust and golden trees await me
in still waters and mountains surrounding.
Porch rockers wave, the crow caws again
flooding my heart with memories
of child-like wonder and days forever lasted.

Down a quiet path I walk,
lined with amber leaves,
dead stem, wild wheat.
This eerie, yet holy place is to be treasured,
this moment to live forever
when I look at my plaid blanket.

Porch Steps

My seat is ice cold
as I watch cars pass by.
The yard exquisite with fallen leaves,
I watch the breeze up high.

This house is small, but full of love.
It inspires, exposes my youthful heart
to mysteries unseen,
of eternal art.

The Old, Gravel Road

Red leaves dance around my feet
in unison with stinging, fall winds
that come so suddenly,
yet are welcomed by my inhaling breath,
and the chill down my back tells me
all is well in this moment.

This morning is sweet, a gift, a joy
that I get to be a part of this majestic
landscape, this small moment
in time of a grand story that is being told, if
we listen.

With a warm cup in hand,
steam becoming the sky,
I gladly walk my gravel road,
with nowhere in particular to go,
but wherever my soul desires,
like by my old, creaky stable
where my heart horses reside.

They prance to the fence line, nickering,
necks curling over me,
eyes so large and kind
with gentle rubs, I see they're art,
a paintbrush stroke from God.

Leaves on a Bridge

I halt at the base,
unsure of what lies ahead.
My mind throws spears of what-ifs
although my heart knows the path.

On this side, I'm familiar,
the far side is unknown,
but imagination shows me
I will not walk alone.

Feed the Fire

I forgot about this place,
where the autumn fog tricks the eye
to think the sun has gone away.

This place, with a dome of bending trees,
that lean in towards me, swaying,

like I'm the only one to be.

Something cracks under my boot,
a familiar, black debris,
of things that burned another time,
faint in memory.

Next to a wood pile
nearly full of rage,
I bend down to grasp
lichen and moss,
and send the fire ablaze.

Never again will I neglect this fire meant to brighten my hardest days.

The Mountain View

Look past the mountain's edge,
of ambrosia red, luscious plum, fiery gold.
Stamp the scene into your mind
let it commune with your soul.

Love is vast and for the taking
written in the way the trees blow,
in the way birds fly,
in the warm light of the sun.

Let's linger awhile,
remember why you're here.
Hear the rocks under your feet,
the silence of the deer.

The Mountains

Trust me, these mountains know you.
You'll find yourself in them.
They'll invite you to know more,
to dip into a forest of creativity.

The mountains will unravel you
from the stressors of this life,
leaving you bare with
peace, kindness, and compassion.
So go claim the tangerine and pink sunsets
behind the rolling hills and peaks.
They were made for you.
The mountains told me.

Beads of Rain

Alone in my room I recover,
listening to beads of rain drip on the glass,
wooing me into a trance full of my past,
the now, and the times ahead.

Somewhere out there is a world I long for,
that will inspire me, where I can grow.
I anticipate the adventure,
my soul quenches it,
I just need to stop worrying so much.

Learn

I forgot how to love myself
It feels impossible to do
I don't think there ever as a time
where I ever had a clue.

I try to compliment myself,
but feel silly doing so.
It's like a hardened heart protects me
of pain from long ago.

Voice deep in the shadows,
critiquing my every move,
I've grown so tired of you now,
I've got nothing left to prove.

I suppose I'll start with a walk
in these amber colored woods.

The Bookstore

There's something about
this autumn day,
sidewalks and brick stained
with rain,
it's like a dream I don't
wish to wake from,
in this erie, yet exciting
way.

That bookstore on the corner
with a paint chipped, red door,
is a small nook filled with vast ideas,
stories from the most beautiful of souls.

I go inside, for I wish to connect,
and what a better way,
to see into the heart of an author,
by the turn of every page.

To fly into new lands,
to see things from another's eyes,
all while in a leather chair, holding
hot coffee, as the busy world goes by.

The Latte

I felt the warm crema as I sipped, gazing quietly out the window. My soul was nourished as I took in this well-crafted cup of perfection on this not so perfect day. It was a fitting companion to my page-turning book and the heavy, puddling rain.

The sizzling and dripping of coffee machines nearby were a sign the day had begun, and all we're focused. An old, grumpy man peering through thick glasses at a newspaper, a young woman buried in a stack of books, a writer nervously clicking away, and a couple across from one another were exchanging loving looks.

Studying my surroundings,
I took another sip. The
bouquet was euphoric, with
a strong fragrance and a
bitter, satisfying taste that
lingered on my lips.

My feet tapped on the oak floors as the soft folk music encompassed the air. My wandering eyes saw people come and go, onto their own affairs.

It felt as if I were in a chapter of a grand story, observing as life around me filled up these cozy walls.

Instantly,
I knew this day was perfect after all.

Fall Market

Nothing fills my soul more
than a crisp, autumn day,
when I'm strolling down a wet road,
in wool and thick plaid,
on my way to the autumn market
to enjoy this season's harvest
of bright pumpkins,
bumpy corn, curling squash,
red and orange mums scattered
throughout town, reaching out
towards us.

Meet Me

Meet me on the mountain,
the one you would only know,
where color hues are rich,
and history sings from long ago.

Meet me on the bridge,
the one blanketed in mauve,
where time fades from the sounds
of our beating hearts in love.

Meet me in the fires
of the golden canopy,
where chills sting my spine
as you hold yourself to me.

Meet me in our bed,
under the window with a view,
of dripping rain and autumn haze,
but pales in
comparison to you.

Candle

A soft flame flickers,
flooding the walls with light,
staining the air with pumpkin
bringing comfort in the night.

We wont go out this evening,
but rather, stay inside,
together we'll wrap up in plaid
and let our dreams collide.

The Wind's Affair

Soft winds,
toying with my thoughts,
luring me, pressing me
to unveil my shielded heart.

You know that i've been hurt
too many times before,
but you will not stop, you will persist,
always wanting more.

Through dawn's waving brush,
or tapping the tips of trees,
or howling down the mountain gorge,
you're there reminding me.

Pouring over the hills ahead,
showing me the way,
with a mighty force
you thrust me
into happy, brighter days.

Night Watch

Glaring one there, blending with the dark.
Are you hunting me or curious
as you stare from afar?

I see those yellow eyes, but not so
when you glide,
through the brush, around the trees,
away from the street lights.

A presence behind me, a breath on my neck,
I turn my head to face you
but alas,
you vanish.

I hear your paws above as
you settle on the roof
on the metal shingles,
claws clink,
ones surely sharp as
scissors.

With a grin and time,
I swing back and forth,
silently awaiting whats next,
then to the side of my eye, a head appears,
from the corner of the rooftop,
a stabbing stare.

We lock eyes, and like a bat you hang lifeless,
studying me to see if I'll bite,
but with a pat on the swing I assure you
I will not.

You leap down next to me,
and purring, shut your eyes,
I pet your head, glad to see you,
and we look into the night.

A New Season

Autumn arrives when things die away,
but my soul comes to life, nourished
by the season's blessings that come
each day, like chilly morning walks,
or gravel crunching at my every step.
I hold myself tight,
in thick plaid and boots, smiling
at the mist of my exhaling breath.

There's something special in the fallen leaves,
the ones blanketed upon
the bone-chilling earth,
coated in raindrops of the night before,
happy to show a new beauty
of crimson and terra-cotta orange,
that follows its inevitable death.

Autumn's presence is homey, rustic,
complete and picturesque
From old, red trucks to hay-filled wagons,
we learn to treasure the little things
during this precious glimpse of heaven.

The smooth feel of pumpkins and gourds
displayed at the corner side market,
the pinecones and acorns people
gather to decorate their homes with,
the cozy scarves and courteroy
flood the sidewalks of the lively town,
while friendly gazes are exchanged
during this time of thanksgiving and harvest.

I reflect on these moments,
as I sit with the golden evening on the
creaky porch, rocking back and forth
in a wool blanket,
the cold air stinging my nose.

I lift my steaming cup in front of me,
gazing into the grey and rust of night,
the smell of apple pie filling my senses
as it trails from the open window,
vanishing into the mountainous sights

I glance over at the old tire swing
where many memories of laughter were shared,
those countless autumns of yellow landscapes
praying I'll see another one again.
Thank you, God, for autumn,
the fingerprint of Your hand.

To practice being present this fall, I will. . .

Go for a hike in the forest.

Made in the USA
Monee, IL
18 September 2023